BRITAIN IN OLD PHOTOGRAPHS

COWES &
EAST COWES

D O N A L D   A .   P A R R

*St Mary's Mission Hall in St Andrews
Street was built in 1886. Today the
building is still being put to good use as
a community centre.*

ALAN SUTTON PUBLISHING LIMITED

Alan Sutton Publishing Limited
Phoenix Mill · Far Thrupp · Stroud
Gloucestershire · GL5 2BU

First published 1995

Copyright © Donald A. Parr, 1995

Cover photographs: (front): Birmingham Road,
Cowes, 1912; (back): Grange School, 1893.

British Library Cataloguing in Publication Data.
A catalogue record for this book is available from
the British Library.

ISBN 0-7509-0939-0

Typeset in 9/10 Sabon.
Typesetting and origination by
Alan Sutton Publishing Limited.
Printed in Great Britain by
Ebenezer Baylis, Worcester.

The launch of the first Princess flying boat from Columbine slipway, East Cowes, took place on 19 August 1952. Although it underwent rigid test flights, this plane, unfortunately, was never put into service.

Contents

Introduction   5

1. Cowes: The People   7

2. Cowes: Sports and Pastimes   27

3. Cowes: Of Ships and the Sea   35

4. Cowes: Around the Town   41

5. Cowes: Places of Worship   57

6. Gurnard and Northwood   65

7. East Cowes: People and Places   73

8. East Cowes: Sports   97

9. East Cowes: Youth Groups   105

10. Royal Osborne   113

11. Whippingham   121

Acknowledgements   126

The Flora Statue now standing in the grounds of Northwood House was unveiled in 1980 by Mr and Mrs Ward, whose family presented it to the council in 1926. Pictured with the statue they so lovingly restored are, left to right: Margaret Lennox, Sharee Hughes, Tony Gildant, -?-, Naomi Ashley, Kirsty Harrower, Katherine Wellstead, and with her hand resting on the statue's arm, Joanne Higginson.

George Gates was a master builder from the late nineteenth century, and his company built a vast number of houses in Cowes, East Cowes and Gurnard. The houses in Pelham Road sold for what was then a high price of £200. Among those pictured in 1912 are George Gates Jnr (in bowler hat), Albert Hodge and William Wyatt.

Introduction

Cowes is one of the main towns of the Isle of Wight – one, however, which is divided by the Island's main river, the Medina, which since 1859 has been spanned by a chain ferry.

Before 1895 both parts of Cowes were known by their geographical locations, West Cowes and East Cowes, but in that year the authorities in West Cowes decided to delete the word 'West' and become known as 'Cowes'. East Cowes, however, retained the geographical adjective. Much friendly rivalry and banter is still exchanged between the two populations: East Cowes people refer to the area across the river as West Cowes, while West Cowes residents in retaliation leave off the 'East'. Thus friendly war is waged.

Both Cowes and East Cowes have always played an equally important part in the success of the Isle of Wight. Both are main ports of entry from Southampton, East Cowes taking over vehicular traffic from Cowes with the introduction of the roll-on roll-off ferries, leaving foot passengers to disembark at Cowes. Also from Cowes, Red Funnel run a fast hydrofoil and jet boat service to the mainland, both taking approximately 20 minutes.

Cowes boasts a number of yacht clubs including the prestigious Royal Yacht Squadron, patronized over the centuries by royalty.

Osborne House, a Palladian mansion designed by Prince Albert, was the family home of Queen Victoria. Its twin towers stand like sentinels overlooking and protecting Osborne Bay. The neatly kept grounds and the house itself are worthy of a visit, and the Queen's private apartments are furnished exactly as she left them.

East and West Cowes have always been the industrial corner of the Island, with ship building, aircraft, flying boat and yacht construction. Sir Christopher Cockerell designed and built the first hovercraft here. It was the home of great companies such as Saunders Roe, which in turn became British Hovercraft (now Westland Aerospace). The ship builders, White's, moved to the Island from Kent in about 1800, and under the patronage of J. Samuel White, whose name the company took, their reputation spread world wide. Unfortunately, like many other shipyards, it was to close in 1965. Elliott Turbomachinery retained the name when they took over the building, but they too closed in 1981. Cowes is also home to a host of internationally known companies such as Ratsey Lapthorne, Spencer Rigging and Souter's – the list is endless – all employing craftsmen of the highest calibre . . .

When dealing with East and West Cowes I have included the outlying villages of Gurnard, Northwood and Whippingham. Once again I am indebted to all those who have loaned me photographs, and to the help and encouragement given by local historians which has made this book possible. As with the first two books I have endeavoured to show the changes that have taken place. In my first book, *Newport in Old Photographs*, the changes are to the town, not affecting many people because of the cosmopolitan nature of the town. My second book, *Around Ryde in Old Photographs*, demonstrates that neither the town nor the nature of the people have changed. This third volume, *Cowes and East Cowes in Old Photographs*, shows great superficial change, caused by the heavy air raids of 1942 and the subsequent changing tide of British industry, but neither has changed the nature of the people. May they never change.

Donald A. Parr
Spring 1995

COWES:

THE PEOPLE

A portrait of the Revd G. Sparks, Baptist minister,

who was born in 1825 and started his ministry

in Cowes in 1866. He worked tirelessly at his

pastoral and civic duties until his retirement

in 1908.

One of the oldest firms in Cowes and still trading is Pascall Atkey, though it is now smaller than the original company. These two photos were taken of the workforce just before the First World War, but unfortunately records are not available to allow the naming of those pictured.

Pascall Atkey were to do their bit for king and country during the First World War by forming their own Volunteer Home Defence force from among the employees. We are only able to name John Cyril Hudson, fourth from the left in the back row. The khaki uniforms are of the 1st Battalion IOW Regt, and the two darker uniforms are of the IOW Rifles.

Ralph Osmond, a Merchant Navy officer, is believed to have lived in Newport Road during the early 1930s.

Thomas William Hudson of Cowes in the uniform of the Volunteer Training Corps, 1915.

Carnivals have been held in Cowes since the late nineteenth century. This is Cowes Carnival in 1956 with Lorna and Robert Hilton as supreme and wise rulers of Kitchenland.

This float was entered by Harry Cheek in the 1945 Cowes Carnival. Harry was the local greengrocer and nurseryman in Northwood. Pictured are Bill Morrell, Harry Cheek, Bob Saunders and Bill Trent.

Cowes Town Band started in the late nineteenth century essentially as a marching band. Many transferred from the Salvation Army band, which then, as now, was renowned for its high standard of brass playing. During both world wars their engagements were cut to a minimum because many members joined the services. This photograph, taken in 1932 outside Northwood House, includes Bill Fripp, 'Art' Dyer, the Revd W. Patterson (Vicar of Holy Trinity Church), Reg Crouch, Jack Britnall, Jimmy Jones, Mr Hoare and Freddy Gibbs (bandmaster).

In 1931 Cowes Town Band was over thirty strong. Here we see Bill Fripp, 'Art' Dyer, Jim Jones, Reg Crouch and Freddy Smart (bandmaster) after a concert in the grounds of Northwood House.

Cowes Salvation Army Band, 1907. Back row, left to right: C. Slade, W. Martin, 'Dad' Blake, W. Carpenter, H. Carpenter, W. Carter, W. Souter, H. Russell. Centre row: F. Martin, S. Burton, B. Payne, A. Adams, A. Davis, B. Powell, F. Wootton, H. Dunford. Front row: C. Burton, W. Chiverton, A. Davis (bandmaster), Mrs Hill, Ensign Hill, W. Duffett, J. Carter, S. Dunford.

Cowes fire station staff, 1958. The photograph includes W. Nicholson, F. White, A. Crisp, L. Richards, W. Morris, M. Jones, T. Slade, J. Greenham, T. Harwood, F. Welland, A. Jacobs, H. Tilbury, W. Smythers, R. Sullivan, B. Gardner and Harry Mundell.

A celebration of an anniversary of the East and West Cowes branch of Vectis Toc H, 1965. Left to right are the Revd John Bean, Bill Faraday, Mrs V. Austin, Mr and Mrs B. Jones (cutting the cake), Harry Burnton and Ron Hilton.

The uniform of the fireman of yesteryear was very different to that of today. Cowes fireman Cy Hardy is seen wearing his large heavy brass helmet in 1898.

This Carisbrooke Castle set was built by G.W. Gates and J.H. Jolliffe for a bazaar at the Wesleyan Sunday School in 1920. Left to right: Capt. Goodwin, Miss A. Underwood, Mrs G.W. Gates, Miss L. Watts, Mrs J.H. Jolliffe, Mr Goodwin, Mr G.W. Gates, J.H. Jolliffe.

The Cowes Amateur Operatic and Dramatic Society (known locally as the CAODS) present *The Rebel Maid* at Alexandra Hall in April 1931. The cast included Roy Highett, John Groves, Norman Telford, Harry Stewart, Henry Butterfield, Jervis Coyney, Graham Stewart, Sydney Sheath, Richard Mason, George McClure, Doreen Knowler, Barbara Burton, Francis Jacobs, Nina Draper and Ida Clamet.

The CAODS gave a performance of *The Country Girl* by Lionel Monkton and Alan Ross, in 1922. Because of the several set changes, this is considered one of the most difficult productions to stage.

HMS Pinafore was performed by the society in 1937. Among the cast were Sidney Rayner, Harry Wellspring, Edgar Manning, Phil Jones, Sydney Sheath, Adrian Scadding, George Waring Jnr, Norah Marshall, Peggy Scadding and Doris Payton.

Yet another performance of the popular classic *The Rebel Maid*, this time in 1948. Ron Hilton and a fellow member of the cast enjoy a cup of tea in the green room.

The CAODS enjoying a well-earned outing after a performance of *Les Cloches de Cornville* in March 1922. The cast included Mrs H. Lallow, Miss F. Brown, Mr S.E. Porter, Mr G. Scadding, Mr H. Butterfield, Mr J. Crossley, Mr F.J. Denham, Master E. Tuffin, Miss E. Tuffin, Mrs S.C. Wadham, Miss Z. Benzie, Mrs J.H. Desmond, Miss M. Batt and Miss T. Brown.

Poppy sellers at the Cowes War Memorial, 1932. The gentleman in the bowler hat is Capt. Adams-Connor, Lord Lieutenant of the Isle of Wight, Chief Constable of the Isle of Wight constabulary and County President of the Royal British Legion.

A group of people on Cowes station, 1948. They are believed to be the host families to Czechoslovakian children who had been staying in Cowes after the war. Included in the picture are Mrs J. Fripp, Mr Bill Fripp, Miss Margaret Fripp and Florrie Rudkins.

Queen Victoria in procession in Cowes High Street during celebrations for her diamond jubilee, July 1897.

Cowes High Street was bedecked with flowers and flags in readiness for the procession. Thousands of Islanders lined the route.

Even after Her Majesty had passed, the crowd still followed their beloved Queen's progress towards The Parade.

On her arrival at Cowes Parade, Her Majesty was unable to view the assembled fleet from her carriage because of the large crowd that had gathered.

We are indebted to former Pascall Atkey employees for allowing us to use these extremely old photographs of Carnival entries. The top picture was taken in Queens Road, probably in 1901. Below is the seafront in 1902.

The removal firm Pickfords, 1905. A team of five horses was used to move a large boiler, difficult for even a modern lorry.

Pickfords parcel service. Mr T.W. Hudson, manager, is third from right.

Dorothy Hounsell with friends Jack and Molly White at the Northwood Tennis Club, 1925.

Denmark Road School, *c.* 1910. The school was demolished in 1990 and is now a car park. We were unable to obtain names of any pupils in the photograph.

Class 4a, Denmark Road School, summer 1962. Back row, left to right: Peter Lambie, Michael Ball, Alan Stroud, William Davis, Michael Matthews, Michael Haywood, Hilary Ash, Lorna Hilton, Sandra Wallace, Pauline Symons, Pamela White. Centre row: Terry Berryman, Helen Webster, Sandra Garwood, Ann Slade, Jacqueline Argles, Sandra Bennett, Jill Farley, Jacqueline Dupree, Stephen Morrison, Alan Wiles, Christine Cox, Adrienne Cork. Front row: Alan Hartley, Christopher Morey, Olive Clayton, Elizabeth Barry, Irene Twort, Wendy Maxted, Allan Merchet, Gordon Chiverton, Maurice Wolcot, David Carmen, John Bowler, Stephen Tutton, Philip Mair. Their teacher is Mr Langride.

Slightly earlier, in 1959, we see Mrs Nash with class 1a. Back row, left to right: Matthew Mair, Kevin Lee, David Hartley, Mark Hilton, David Ainsworth, Jean Brett, Jennifer Russell, Gillian Read, Tony Martin, John Lock, Ian ?, Steven Spencer. Centre row: Kay Starke, Melvin Beale, Carol Pugsley, Alan Perkins, Lesley Arnell, Allan Luff, Susan Matthews, Robert ?, Lindsay Pilbeam. Front row: Susan Warder, Leonard Pullinger, Joy Crouch, David Chapman, Julia Furley, John Rosenthal, Lesley Stillwell, Ian ?, Susan Chivers, Peter ?, Christine ?.

Love Lane School pupils, with teacher Vera Taylor, set out to discover the whereabouts of the Flora Statue which for many years had stood on the green. Found in a room at Northwood House, it had been stored there for safety during the Second World War. With the help of many local people the children restored it (see page 4). 'The Flora' was first presented to Cowes by the nephew of George Stephenson (of 'Rocket' fame) to commemorate the marriage of the Prince of Wales to Princess Alexandra. To mark the unveiling, many activities took place including maypole dancing. The picture above shows teachers Gill Coles (in black) and Monica Brooks; below are, left to right, Katherine Wellstead, Ruth Brannagh, Naomi Ashley and Paula Rawlings.

York Street infant school, 1941. It seems that, in common with most schools in Cowes, York Street came under the hammer of the planners and was demolished in the early 1960s. Houses now stand on the site.

The Grange was originally a large private house in Baring Road; it was used from 1893 to 1902 as a private school.

Section Two

COWES: SPORTS AND PASTIMES

Northwood Cricket Club pavilion, 1928. It was

destroyed in an air raid during the Second World

War.

Cowes Football Club, winners of Hampshire Senior Cup, 1945/6. Back row, left to right: L.G. Burton (Trainer), J. Eckford, A. Duffield (Capt.), P. Board, E. Hayter, D. Bradford, R. Baskett, E. Hutchings (Assistant Trainer). Front row: R. Jones, S. Hooper, J. Shergold, C. Lonnon, L. Laney.

Cowes Football Club, first winners of the Hampshire Shield and winners of the Hampshire Senior Cup, 1897. Back row: C. Sibbick, W. Mouncher, W. Pickford, H. Wall, Dr W. Hoffmeister (President), J. McKenzie, C. Cooper, F. Lock (Sec.) and A. Wolcott. Third row: C. Deacon, A. Clark, Sgt McLaughlin, J. Nesbett, R. Hammet, C. Ward, A. Wilson, H. Moore. Second row: J. Ronald (Assistant Trainer), L. Thomson, R. McCrindle, J. Jolliffe, J. Black (Trainer). Front row: W. Fryer, A. Baker, E. Baker, D. Dean, C. Samuel, F. Moore, A. Fellows.

Cowes Cross Street School football team, winners of the Isle of Wight School Shield, 1936/7 season. Back row, left to right: T. Egan, Mr R. Cutten, E. Wheatley, J. Holmes, R. Niell, C. Spencer, Mr Barton (Headmaster), A. Taylor. Seated: A. Reed, J. Harrigan, N. Spence, J. Williams, E. Barsy.

In the 1919/20 season an Isle of Wight Memorial Cup competition was inaugurated. It was won by East Cowes Vics, who also won the Challenge Cup. Included are ? Tong, ? Searle, ? Brown, Bill Chindin, ? Stroud, D. Wheeler, L. Lambet, ? Tutton, ? Hales, G. Jago, W. Mogar, J. Cox, H. Martin, W. Streets, P. Coffin, F. Reed, ? Tong, R. Downer, P. Robinson, J. Roy, ? Bell, J. Hales, V. House, J. Roberts, H. Mathers, H. Mogar, A. Todman, ? Bennett, C. Oatley, E. Bennett, G. Paddock, ? Fish, J. Hunt, ? Quelch, S. Cooper and ? Caribou.

No book featuring Cowes football teams could be complete without mentioning 4 May 1912, when Cowes, spurred on by their supporters, beat Southampton by one goal to nil in the Hants Senior Cup.

Cowes Football Club, winners of the Gold Cup in 1950/1. The club officials shown here are H. Jones, J. Berryman, R. King, J. White, J. Matthews, C. Fellows, G. Holder, L. Varney, R. Gladdis, L. Burton (Trainer), T. Paul (Assistant Secretary), B. Moore, R. Irwin (Treasurer), J. Woolacott, R. Reynolds (Secretary), W. Cheek (Chairman), and S. Jones (President). The players are A. Stratta, J. Salter, D. Cameron, W. Bushby, J. Ship, A. Roles, W. Beavis, N. Mignot, G. Rice, B. Johnstone and L. Laney, and their mascot is R. Lashmar.

Cowes Rifle Club after their annual shoot, 1920. This group includes T.W. Hudson, R. Floyd, J.C. Hudson, E. Rogers, Mr Morey, Mr and Mrs Edward Jones, Mr Gladdis, Mrs Morey, Mrs Rhodes, Miss Floyd, Miss Brinton. In the front row are George Matthews, Cyril Rhodes, Sidney Rhodes, Miss Matthews and George Matthews Jnr.

In 1920 Cowes Rifle Club had their ranges at Westwood Grounds. Included here are John Cyril Hudson, Edward Jones and Thomas William Hudson (Hon. Sec.).

Cowes Rifle Club, winners of the 'Ralli' Cup, 1920. Back row, left to right: H. Lee, T.W. Hudson (Hon. Sec.). Front row: G. Matthews, E. Rogers, E. Jones, R. Floyd.

Northwood Cricket Club pictured outside their pavilion, 1904. Back row, left to right: E. Mouncher (Umpire), P. Shergold, W. Nobbs, A. Hammer, P. Jefferies, F. Moore, Sam Griffin (Scorer). Seated: Alec Stephenson, ? Damant, C. Howell, Arthur White, Arthur Watson, J.C.W. Damant.

During the Second World War, Saunders Roe were to build two-man commando canoes. In 1979 two of the apprentices, Andrew Baxter and Gary Jones, decided to take on as a project the refurbishment of one of these special operations canoes.

Northwood Cricket Club, 1902. Back row, left to right: T. Westbrooke, E. Turley, A. Fellows, H.J. Matthews, F.G. White (Hon. Sec.). Seated: J.W. Shergold, F. Moore, A. Hammer, Res McCarthy, C. Matthews. Seated on grass: P. Jefferies, W. Nobbs.

The 7th Cowes Methodist Scouts at camp, 1953. Back row, left to right: Rickman, Hash, Heatherington, Ward, Munroe, Head. Second row: Martin, Hinton, Floyd, Jones, Groves, Dominey. Front row: Jones, Ralph, Hinton, Harrison, Yarranton, Ward.

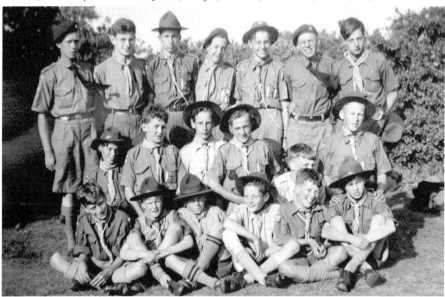

The 7th Cowes Methodist Scout Group was warranted on 1 April 1944. This is the all-Island Scout camp, which was held at Corf in 1950. Back row, left to right: Stubbs, Warner, Willis, Ouhsworth, Peach, Woods, Rickman. Second row: Munroe, Granger, Yarranton, Martin, Flower, Tutton. Front row: Butcher, Barry, Denham, Lee, Taylor, Matthews.

COWES: OF SHIPS
AND THE SEA

RMS Olympic, *sister ship to the ill-fated* Titanic,
passing the Royal Yacht Squadron, 1932.

Queen Victoria's favourite Royal Yacht, *Victoria and Albert II*, was launched at Pembroke in 1855. She was a two-funnelled paddle steamer, 300 ft long, with a 40 ft beam and a displacement of 2,470 tons. *Victoria and Albert II* was broken up in 1904, three years after the Queen's death.

J. Samuel White & Co. boasted a huge export order book. The *Sarota* was built by them for Crown Agents to be used in Northern Nigeria. *Sarota* was a stern wheel steam ship 135ft in length, and is pictured here in 1902.

The Polish ship ORP *Blyskawica* was built at Cowes in the late 1930s by J. Samuel White & Co. On the night of 12 May 1942 she was to play a decisive role in saving the town of Cowes. It was during a heavy raid when over 200 tons of high explosive was dropped on the area that the crew of *Blyskawica* were to fight tirelessly throughout the night. At one point cold water was sprayed on her gun barrels to save them from overheating.

Cowes sea front, 1884. This was before the building of The Parade, and would be unrecognizable to residents today – although many of the buildings remain intact.

The River Medina, 1953. This shows the west bank including the gantry crane, a familiar landmark to all entering Cowes from the sea.

Built by J. Samuel White & Co. and launched on 28 June 1916, HMS *Sable* was an 'R'-class destroyer. Her length was 265 ft.

Cowes Parade from the pier. The elegant Victorian terrace in the background was demolished in 1929, before Osborne Court was built.

The freehold of the ground of Cowes Castle was purchased by the Royal Yacht Squadron in 1917. It is here that the guns from the *Royal Adelaide*, King William IV's yacht, now stand. They were presented by Edward, Prince of Wales in 1877, and from these battlements King George VI stood to salute the armada of ships as they sailed for the D-Day landings.

These two aerial views of Cowes are worth studying. The top one shows the River Medina and the Hampshire coast. The picture below shows one of the old Red Funnel steamers moored alongside the pier at Fountain Quay in 1938.

COWES: AROUND THE TOWN

Cowes windmill, from a drawing by E. Wyatt.

Bannisters was established as a company in 1820 and became a subsidiary of J. Samuel White in 1957. The firm was a world leader in the manufacture of ropes and sheets for ships such as the racing yacht *Britannia* and HMS *Victory*.

The rope-making machinery, installed as early as 1904, was in a long passageway named the Rope Walk, which was 1,000 ft long and 3 ft wide. The factory and rope walk were demolished in 1967.

These two photographs show the devastation caused by the fire at J. Samuel White's machine shop on a night in early 1911. Fire crews attended from all parts of the Island but were unable to save the building. Even the Osborne apprentices turned out with their own fire pump. The devastation extended from Thetis Road to Medina Road.

The Cowes Pontoon has for many years been the main point of entry for visitors to the town. If we compare the photo taken in 1911 (above) with the scene in 1959 (below) we can see what has changed.

The gateway to Northwood House, known as Park Gate, 1933. This gate has now been demolished.

Promenaders out for a casual summer afternoon stroll past Cowes Green, July 1907. Next to the bandstand is the Flora Statue.

The Vectis Bus Company garage, Somerton, 1921. The buses are, left to right, DL 2446, DL 2447, DL 2491 and DL 2448, all Isle of Wight registration numbers. The site which became Somerton Airport is now occupied by Siemens Plessey Radar.

These two buses, ADL 500 and ADL 501, were the first true double-decker buses on the Isle of Wight, being Dennis Lances. They seated fifty-six people, and were introduced in 1936.

Cowes War Memorial stood in the centre of the road at the junction of Market Hill and the High Street. It was slightly damaged during the Second World War and was moved for safety to Northwood Park, where it still stands.

Mill Hill Road, Cowes, 1920. This shows the remains of the old mill which once stood and worked on this site.

Little has changed in the bottom half of Cowes High Street, as can be seen from this picture dated 1902.

Cowes High Street, probably 1923. Even in those days two-way traffic must have presented problems.

Another view of the High Street, date unknown. Clearly shown is S.D. Cawill's shop.

The Clarendon Restaurant opposite the pontoon, 1919. The restaurant belonged to Edward Mew of Porchfield and was one of the most popular in the town. Unfortunately it closed in 1931. Pictured in the doorway are Mary Mew (wife), Ethel Mew (daughter) and their dog, Bob.

Before the Second World War, the War Memorial was a proud monument to those of Cowes who fell in the First World War.

The Royal Marine Hotel in its heyday, *c.* 1910. On the right is the gatehouse to Cowes Castle, home of The Royal Yacht Squadron.

Cowes firemen on The Parade showing the canvas rescue chute, 1899. Mr Whittington is holding the horse. On a call out he would approach Mr Gange, a local businessman of Park Road, for the loan of his horse. If Mr Gange decided that the horse was tired after a hard day, he had been known to refuse.

When the railways decided that they should modernize in the 1930s, existing coaches had to be transported from the mainland to Cowes. Island cranes were unable to deal with the weight, so a floating crane accompanied the rolling stock to offload it on to the lines of the Island railways.

The train from Newport arriving at Cowes station, 1922. On leaving Newport it would call at the Cement Mills Halt and Mill Hill station before travelling through the tunnel to Cowes.

The railway played an important part in linking Cowes with other major Island towns. Many Cowes residents will look back nostalgically on a train with a full head of steam heading for Newport in 1943.

The railway also played a large part in the economy of the Island. Barges would bring coal to Cowes to be loaded into trucks at the Medham sidings.

Though not directly connected to the ferry terminal at Cowes pontoon, trains played a leading role in transporting many thousands of holiday-makers and residents to various Island destinations. After discharging their passengers, they would reverse, uncouple the engine and re-couple to the opposite end for the return journey.

Birmingham Road, Cowes, 1912. The small boy nearest the shop is thought to be Bert Jones. It is hard to believe that the Birmingham Road we know today was once used by stagecoaches.

Cowes station entrance. As the railway terminus was higher than the road, the approach was via a set of steps at the side of the buildings.

Alexander Hall in Birmingham Road was the second theatre used by the Cowes Amateur Operatic and Dramatic Society and was to remain their home from 1911 until 1939. One of the last performances in that year was *The Gondoliers* by Gilbert and Sullivan.

Medina Road would often flood on the spring tides. Most of the buildings shown in this photograph have now been demolished, and the road has taken on an entirely different appearance.

The Princess flying boat was first conceived in 1947 and made her first flight in August 1952. Originally an order for three had been placed by BOAC, but this was revoked in early 1951. It was then thought that the RAF would be interested in the plane for use as long-range military transport, but this too came to nothing. The second and third planes were cocooned in a film of plastic until suitable use could be found for them – but this never materialized, due to a change of policy.

COWES: PLACES
OF WORSHIP

The Revd Colin Trenchard Carre, first Priest in
Charge of All Saints', Gurnard, after the forma-
tion of the Conventional District, affording the
church full parish status, in the 1920s.

When the Baptist Church was first planned a group of future parishioners decided that they would build it themselves. Unfortunately their names have vanished into the mists of time, but we have this photograph, dated 1867, showing them on the church steps.

Above left: The Revd Thomas Mann was appointed to the Sun Hill Congregational Ministry in 1822. Through his efforts the church was enlarged and a new organ installed in 1839. Mr Mann retired in 1864 after over forty years of service. *Above right*: Sun Hill Congregational Church was closed in 1969 because of structural defects and services were transferred to the Sunday school building. The church was finally sold in 1971.

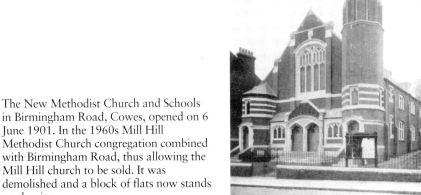

The New Methodist Church and Schools in Birmingham Road, Cowes, opened on 6 June 1901. In the 1960s Mill Hill Methodist Church congregation combined with Birmingham Road, thus allowing the Mill Hill church to be sold. It was demolished and a block of flats now stands on the site.

Cowes Baptist Church on its completion, 1868. The building of the church was instigated by the Revd G. Sparks, who was the first pastor and remained for forty-one years. During that time he became a member of the town council, and a plaque that commemorates his civic work can be seen set into the wall along the esplanade.

The church had a face-lift and was decorated with floral gifts for the diamond jubilee service in 1927. The Revd H. Carter officiated.

For many years there has been a strong Methodist influence in Cowes with churches at Birmingham Road and Mill Hill Road. Mr Phillips of Pallance Road was noted for holding events in the grounds of his large home, 'Woodside', and for entertaining the Methodist Circuit ministers. The photograph above, taken in 1940, includes the following ministers: Mr Rand (Mill Hill), Mr Clifford, Mr A.J. Perry (Birmingham Road), Mr Hammond and Mr Franklin. The photograph below, dating from 1960, shows (back row): Mr Christian, Mr Henry, Mr Parsons, Mr Creamer, Mr Gentle; and (front row): Mr MacLean, Mr Milden and Mr Clarke.

The Roman Catholic Church, St Thomas of Canterbury, 1943. This church has always had a strong following in Cowes. The school next to the church building was one of the main places of learning with the introduction of full-time state education.

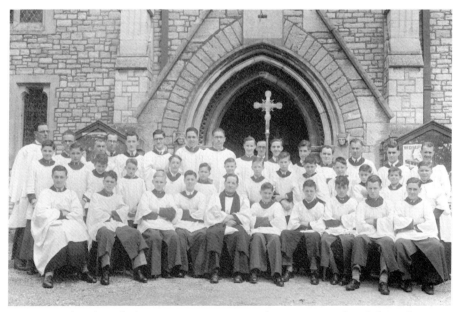

St Mary's Church and choir, June 1947. Pictured are Mr Bromley, Sid Hayles, Ron Hilton, Ray Hayter, Mr Lovelace, Wilf King (Choirmaster), ? Cox, ? Biddlecombe, ? Pelham, ? Rodley, P. Smart, S. Smart, the Revd Mr Crewe and John Parsons.

The Sunday School Council of the Victoria Wesleyan Methodist Church, Cowes, Northwood Park, 16 July 1913. Back row, left to right: A. Hillyear, F.J. Phillips, W. Smart, P. Jackman, J.W. Brown, J. Phillips, P. Richards, A. Booker, W. Russell. Fourth row: A. Messenger, R. Rogers, J.H. Jolliffe, F. White, D. Jolliffe, S. Watts, J. Warne, G. Attrill, C. Wiggins, S. Warne, W. Sargent, S. Long, A. Ward, H. Corke, F.J. Potter. Third row: A.S. Ford, R. Newman, E. Underwood, H. Hodge, S. Jolliffe, Jesse Jolliffe, Henry Munt, Miss L. Munt, Mrs D. Jolliffe, Miss N. Hodges, Miss T. Sargeant, Miss D. Booker, Miss M. Jolliffe, H.H. Perry Jnr, G.W. Ball, H. Payne. Second row: A. Debenham, N. Phillips, H. Beale, H.H. Munt, 'Arch' Jolliffe, W. Munt, J.A. Susans, Revd F. Boden, Alfred Jolliffe, G. Gates, Mrs H.H. Perry, Mrs W. Rolf, Miss M. Hamilton, Mrs G. Gates, Mrs P. Jackman, Mrs S. Long, Mr H.H. Perry. Front row: Miss E. Bilk, Mrs A. Messenger, Miss E. Brown, Miss E. Higham, Miss B. Jackman, Miss A. Underwood, Mrs J.A. Susans, Miss H.E. Perry, Mrs J.H. Jolliffe, Miss J. Campbell, Mrs A. Jolliffe, Miss E. Watts, Miss F. Watts, Miss L. Watts, Miss E. Wiggens.

The combined Methodist churches in Cowes have always had a strong following at their sisterhood meetings. This photograph shows an outing of the Cowes Methodist Sisterhood in 1936.

All Saints' Church, Gurnard, Summer Fête, 14 August 1934. The second clergyman on the left is the Revd L. Greenham. Next to him, in white trousers with a yachting cap, is the Revd G. Patterson from Holy Trinity Church, Cowes.

GURNARD AND
NORTHWOOD

7th Northwood Scouts HQ with Vic Hansford,

who made the gates and carved the badge, and

Arch Whitcombe, who helped to erect the hut and

lay the drive. The hut was burned down in

November 1962.

Lord Rowallan meets Lou Rosenthal when he was on a visit to the Island Scouts at Northwood, 1928.

Phoebe Raddings, one of the Island Hon. Commissioners of Cubs who was an active member of the movement until she retired at the age of seventy. She is pictured with Sir Charles MacLean, Chief Scout, and Scout Officer Jim Goad at Corf Camp in 1969.

7th Northwood Scouts on weekend camp, August 1926. On this photograph are A. Day, J. Reed, B. Morrall, K. Hayward, S. Gustar, R. Gustar, A. Warek, R. Westmore, A. Ball, L. Varney, N. Rose, D. Rise, D. Riddett and C. Gladdis.

The inauguration of the Southampton to Cowes airline at Somerton Airport, May 1949. Those in the picture include Councillor Joseph Frank Sinclair (Chairman of Cowes Town Council) and his wife, Jimmy Raddings, Brig. Robin Hutchins, Leslie Baines and representatives from the police, the Fleet Air Arm and the RAF.

Jimmy and Phoebe Raddings with their dog Liebling stand next to their Auster Autocrat aircraft at Somerton Airport, 1950.

Arthur George Harwood was the licensee of the Horseshoe Inn at Northwood from 1922, and remained there for thirty-eight years. Arthur and his wife Jessica are pictured on their retirement in 1960.

Arthur and Jessica celebrated their Golden Wedding in 1959. They are seen here with their children. Left to right: Ted, Arthur William, Kathleen, Pamela, Arthur George, Jessica, Patricia, Jack, Tony (Bert), Vic.

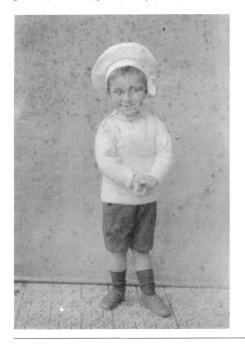

Arthur William Harwood on his fourth birthday, 1910.

This photo of the Horseshoe Inn was sent to Arthur William by his mother Jessica in 1945. At the time he was in the South Pacific serving on board the aircraft carrier HMS *Striker*.

This rare photograph of Gurnard front was taken in 1930 when visitors and residents alike flocked to the beach. Today Gurnard, in common with other resorts, plays host to fewer visitors but still retains a peaceful old-world charm.

All Saints' Church, Gurnard, 1912.

The Revd Charles Frederick Aspinwall with the choir of All Saints' Church, 1943. It is interesting to note that the choir members are all girls, unusual at that time, when females in choirs were usually adults.

EAST COWES:
PEOPLE AND PLACES

The Town Hall was donated to East Cowes Urban District Council on 27 March 1897

by Mrs J.S. White. At one time it was due to become part of the grand scheme known as

East Cowes Park, but unfortunately this was never completed. With the amalgamation in

1933 of East and West Cowes, the town hall became redundant but has since had many

uses, from the staging of dances and dramatics to amateur boxing, while today it is the

local community centre.

The first hydro-aeroplane, built at East Cowes by J. Samuel White & Co., 1912. She is seen here at her launch on 5 May 1913. Unfortunately, just eight days later on 13 May she was wrecked.

The Saunders Roe Princess Flying Boat on one of her test flights over the Island, 1952. This beautiful gentle giant was the world's largest all-metal flying boat.

Another of the achievements of Saunders Roe was the Bat Boat, their first amphibious aircraft, which was built in 1912.

The SRN 1. The first amphibious hovercraft, before the fitting of rubber skirts, being tested in 1959.

The SRN 1, prototype of the modern hovercraft, preparing for her maiden channel crossing in 1959. At the helm is test pilot Peter Lamb.

Since the first appearance of the hovercraft, each successive model brought with it new wonders. The SRN 4 on her roll-out day in the early 1960s was no exception.

In 1924 severe flooding hit East Cowes. As the picture above shows, help was at hand for those who needed it. The picture below is of a fruit and veg. lorry making its belated way along the street to deliver its cargo. It was late afternoon before traffic could once again use the High Street.

Mr William Brading, founder of W.H. Brading and Son, Building Contractors and Ships' Joiners, with his wife Lydia, 1909.

Dorothy Hounsell and her friend Eileen Caws at the East Cowes Tennis Club, 1915. The club was situated in a field near Norris Castle.

Brading Wharf, as the name suggests, was owned by W.H. Brading and Son. Their position on the river gave good facilities for repairing and painting the many yachts that visited Cowes.

FRONT

BED AND
BREAKFAST

TEA GARDEN

THE SHELL HOUSE

SHOP

35 CAMBRIDGE ROAD
EAST COWES
I.W.

GARDEN WALK

These two postcards show eight views between them. The card above was produced by the owners of The Shell House. More details will be found on page 82. The card below shows Sheddon Esplanade, opened in 1924. Details of this are on page 83.

Edward Sibbick with two of his workmen, Sam Williams and Arthur ? in 1910, just before the houses in St Davids Road were completed.

At the end of the Second World War street parties were held in most towns up and down the British Isles. East Cowes was no exception, and here we see the VE-day party in full swing in St Davids Road.

Kingston Power Station, 1932. It was the sole supplier of electricity for the Island.

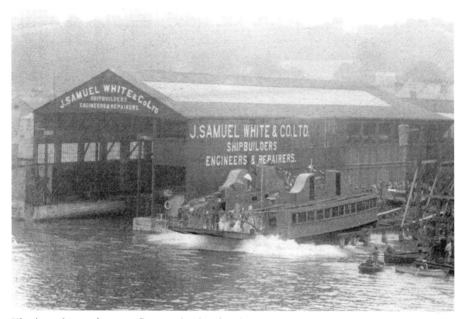

The launching of a new floating bridge for the East to West Cowes chain ferry by J.S. White's at their East Cowes Yard, 12 May 1936. The large building was known as the submarine shed.

The Shell House in Cambridge Road was presented to William Attrill by Queen Victoria as a wedding present. Her Majesty had never forgotten William for the occasion when he blacked the eye of the Prince of Wales, later to become Edward VII. As a boy William Attrill sold periwinkles from a site on Cowes Green. The Prince of Wales said that they were offensive to the aristocratic air of Cowes, kicked over the basket and ran away. Attrill gave chase, caught him and gave him a black eye. On hearing this Queen Victoria said that he thoroughly deserved it. In gratitude, William Attrill decorated the house with shells collected from the beach and continued to do so until his death in 1926. The Shell House became such an attraction that postcards were sold to holiday-makers.

The tug *Dwulia* towing the *Medway Queen* into the mouth of the Medina on the way to her moorings at Cowes Haven, 1964. She was to remain here as a night club and floating bar for many years, before being returned to Chatham for restoration and permanent moorings.

This esplanade was opened in 1924. Mr George Sheddon of Spring Hill donated the land to help relieve unemployment; the East Cowes Urban District Council paid the men to create the esplanade. A plaque to commemorate this is on the wall before Shore Cottage. The esplanade runs from the town to the boundaries of Norris Castle Estate. In 1925 a paddling pool was added.

After being launched by J. Samuel White, ships would be manoeuvred over to the west bank, known as 'F.O.B.', ready for finishing. This photograph dates from 1929/30.

The ship in J. Samuel White's stocks is the *Mermaid*, a light-house boat built for Trinity House. Her length was 221 ft. She is pictured just before her launch on 26 March 1959.

Grange Road School, 1911. Over the years it has been a place of learning for most of the inhabitants of East Cowes, and has produced some of the finest sports teams in the school circuit.

Miss Stevens' class at East Cowes infants school, 1909. Included here are Miss Stevens, L. Barnes, J. Oatley, L. Attrill, S. Aitken, L. Fryer, A. Fryer, A. Sinnicks, O. Board, W. Millmore, D. Morey, B. Suter, L. Barrett, C. Board, R. Millmore, F. Suter, R. Blake and F. Benton.

Churchwardens and sidesmen of St James' Church, East Cowes, 1950. Back row, left to right: -?-, Mrs Board, Mr F. Petty Jnr, F. Daltry, ? Brinton, ? Saunders. Second row: ? Brading, ? Jackman, G. Jones, -?-, ? Shave, ? Jackman, D. Brinton, A. Board, F. Petty. Front row: ? Knapp, P. Saunders, the Revd Mr King, H. Brading, Mr Tong.

Paul Pearson, second projectionist, in the projection room of the Kings Cinema, East Cowes, 1937. Paul later became senior projectionist at the Medina Cinema, Newport. During the war he served in the RAF.

The Bishop of Portsmouth, Dr Neville Lovett, consecrating new burial grounds at East Cowes Cemetery, November 1932. Among those present were Messrs J. Taylor and H.W. Brading (Churchwardens), E.J. Bechervaise, Diocesan Registrar, the Revd C.S. Stooks, the Revd Dr R. McKew CBE, the Revd Dr R.S. Moxon, the Revd G. Mostyn Pritchard, and the Revd Peter Duke-Baker. Messrs A. Sibbick (Chairman), C. Leal, G.J. Mason and J.S. Knight (Clerk) represented the UDC.

The 1st East Cowes Girls Brigade Co. Carnival Float portraying Grace Darling, 1953. On the float, from left to right, are Rosemary Brown, Annis Dibbens, Gwen Cruise, Mary Hollis, Eileen Cruise and Val Attrill. In the background is Osborne Road School.

The wedding of George and Florrie Weeks, 1920. Standing, left to right: George Weeks Snr, George Jnr, Florrie's father. Front row: Maisie, Florrie, Barbara. During the early part of the century the Weeks family were proprietors of a general store in East Cowes. By appointment to the Royal Family, they supplied the royal barges.

Dorothy and Alan Weeks with their two children Christopher and Sally, 1940. Alan taught at Denmark Road School and was known by the nickname 'Nana', and Dorothy was head of Grange Road School. Christopher is now working and living in France and Sally is a doctor in Canada.

Grandfather Weeks at home with his family at The Limes, Cambridge Road, 1895. Grandfather (back row, leaning against the post) was private secretary to Mr John Samuel White. Pictured are Nellie (with dog), Minni, George, Blanch, Fanny, Ralph and Eddy, Alan, Mum and Dad (sitting at back) and Hubert, guarding the family parrot. The Limes was destroyed during the Second World War after sustaining a direct hit.

J.S. White Jubilee, 1948. Standing, left to right: G.W. Palferman, W. Souter, A. Hoare OBE, R. Royle, H.G. Cameron, H.J. Butcher, S. Rose, F.S. Billowes MBE, A.C. Brading MBE, W. Corney, T.P. Adams, J. Mullock, R. Cousland OBE, A. Coleman, A. Allemande, G. Scadding. Seated: F. Tiltman, R. Allen, C. Bettenson, F. Shearman, J. Attrill, Sir James A. Milne CBE, G. Fardell, A. Rowe, S.G. Carnt, H. Fox, Admiral H. Perring.

The amusement committee of the East Cowes UDC at a fête, 1932. Left to right: A.F. Sibbick (Chairman), Charlie Leal (in box), -?-, George Joyce, George Mason.

The Saunders Roe canteen staff, 1940. Among those in the group, photographed in the company grounds, are Ena Gough, Joy Eldridge, Violet Plumley, Mr Gold, Mr Hayward Joan Bruce, Mrs Cook, Phil Read, Eva Michelmore, Mrs Chapman, Mrs Flux, Mrs Wirth, Mrs Bishop, Minnie 'Ha-ha', Amy ?, Mrs Gatton, Elsie Chiverton, Iris ?, Jean Morrell, Mrs Bruce and Olive Kelly.

Arthur Shearing and his fellow fireman standing by their steam pump tender at East Cowes, 1907.

East Cowes Infant School, 1920. Among the pupils are Betty Church, Alan Dexter, Roy Street, Bill March, Bill Davies, ? Stevens, Dorothy Parsons, Dorothy Arnold, Gilbert James, Margaret Herbert, Alan Ford, ? Orchard, Bill South, Phyllis Sinnicks, Bill Moth, Olive Blake, ? Corny, Jocelyn Hendy, Betty Ford, Norah Nicholson, Peggy Snudden, Sylvia Barton, Ted Reed, Marjorie Lawrence and Eric Tiltman. Their teacher is Mrs Ford.

Shipyard staff, J.S. White, Cowes, 1938. Back row, left to right: E. Attrill, H. Elliott, R. Elderfield, F. Colnutt, W. Thorburn, S. McClean, E. Cook, -?-, S. Clark, H. Bracegirdle, G. Mason, B. Roy. Second row: P.C. Jacobs, T. Foster, C. Reid, C. Saunders, D. Corney, -?-, W. Scardifield, A. Carpenter, F. Tiltman, E. Moore, J. Etherington, M. Hodges. Front row: A. Craig, -?-, S. Caunter, W. Smith, R. Cousland, Mr Hodges, A. Brading, -?-, -?-, J. Parker, Mr Southcot.

Falcon shipyard drawing office staff, 1906. Back row, left to right: Mr P. Hastie, T. Bulled, R. Smith, A.C. Brading, G.W. Rowe, J. Blake, R. Tupman, A.O. Thompson, C. Simpson. Front row: C. Thomas, Mr Elliston, W. White, J. Moffet, A. Charleston, G. Dymott, C. Watts, R. Smith, O. Hounsell, T. Harvey.

Frank James hospital was originally a home for seamen, built in the nineteenth century by the two James brothers in memory of their third brother Frank, a serving sailor who was killed by an elephant in Africa. The running of it was financed by donations from local people and the Osborne Naval College. Earlier this century it was converted into a hospital.

The Millmore family from Yarborough Road, East Cowes, 1910. Most of them worked at J. Samuel White & Co. The family group includes Charlie, Beatie, Lucy (mother), Ronald, William and Dorothy.

The East Cowes Civil Defence first aid party at Kent House, headquarters of the rescue party during the Second World War. Standing, left to right: -?-, Roy, Steed, Tiltman, Maegek, Chambers, -?-, South, Watts, Washbrook. Seated: Simpson, Raper, Walkinshaw, Old, Small. Absent members of the team were Polly, Capps, Groves and Brownhill.

Refuse collection has always been a problem. Here we see Mr A.E. Sibbick with his steam traction engine in 1910, collecting the East Cowes rubbish. Mr Presseyt and Arthur Cross are also present.

The Floating Bridge taking passengers and carriages for the trip across the River Medina from East to West Cowes, 1906.

Section Eight

EAST COWES: SPORTS

Saunders Roe apprentices sports club entered many

local competitions. In 1955 apprentices

D. Halliday, B. Simmonds, B. Martin,

E. Pinchin, R. George and D. Peters won the Isle

of Wight Senior Six-a-Side Football Tournament.

The apprentices club had a strong rowing team and in their gigs named *Ebb* and *Flow* would often compete against such firms as Groves and Gutteridge. In 1956 the team, comprising D. Halliday (No. 3), D. Head (No. 2), K. Sexton (Stroke), J. Arnold (Cox) and D. Ireson (Bow) won the Cowes 'Head of the River' competition.

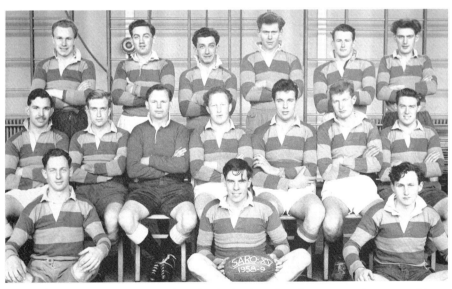

Although not a major sport on the Island, the Saunders Roe apprentices were able to field a strong rugby team for 1958/9. Back row, left to right: J. Farthing, D. Head, D. Halliday, K. Watson, A. Thorpe, N. Westmore. Second row: R. Pink, J. Breaks, R. Jones (Coach), D. Jones (Captain), G. Stables, R. Abell, K. Sexton. Front row: M. Marchant, B. Drake, M. Fitzpatrick-Robertson.

East Cowes Nomads was formed from those unable to make the first team. This is the team for the 1944/5 season. Back row, left to right: Ken Calton, -?-, George Marvin, Jack Riddell (Trainer). Second row: Arthur Grant, Doug Jones, Bill South. Front row: Bert Harvey, Bob Butler, Willie Woolwebber, Harold Bracegirdle, -?-.

Saunders Roe Sports Day, 1938. Included here are Mollie Vine, June Vine, Joan Lister, Jeanne Graines, Rosetta Brading, Grace Hobby, Peter J. Taylor, Peggy Maskell, Ray Durrell, Betty Vine, Marjorie Groves, Audrey Young, Doris Power, Ruby Bennett, Pat Halliday, John McGarity, Dorothy Parsons, Pat Chapman, Leon Stewart, Belle Endersby, Molly Jones, Pat Narder, Wendy Juby and Stella Calton.

Football League Champions and Cup Winners together with the Netball Tournament Winners, Grange Road School, 1959/60. Back row, left to right: Mr Wileman, B. Morey (with cup), J. Welsh, S. Buckell, J. Loveless, T. Bradley, B. Elliott, M. Pearce, D. Elsom, G. Hall (with cup), Mrs Weeks. Centre row: M. Mulcock, S. Harvey, K. Ford, S. Morey, Miss Thorne, G. Mitchell, J. Impey, B. Luckney, R. Sharp. Front row: A. Young, P. Ellis, P. Woolford (with ball), R. McCully, J. Lyness.

The 1921/2 Grange Road School Football Team was unbeaten in every competition it entered during that season.

East Cowes Cricket First Eleven, 1950. Back row, left to right: -?-, Bill South, Don Pragnell, -?-, Dave Aitkin, Albert Weeks, Doug Jones, Jim Sansom, Cecil Cave, John Davies, Dick Cogger (Umpire). Front row: Bill Medley (Treasurer), Eric Nash, Oscar Board (Captain), Roy Bundy, Sid Simpson, Cecil Griames (Secretary).

Football team, East Cowes, April 1921. Included here are the trainer, Mr Goater with his dog, Mr Welch, ? Floyd, ? White, Mr Williams, ? Kingswell, A. Floyd, ? Deacon, ? Day, ? Ketchell, ? Pearce and ? Venables (Captain).

East Cowes Vics were to win the Isle of Wight League Second Division in the 1906/7 season. Back row, left to right: E. Hayles, A. Knapp, V. Knapp, W. Smith, F. Wavell. Centre row: G. Lane, F. Morey, S. Steen (Captain), H. Long. Front row: T. Betterson, A. Chandler, G. Bennett, A. Clarke, B. Barton.

East Cowes Vics first team, Hampshire League Third Division winners, 1947/8 season. Standing, left to right: George Elliot (Secretary), Eric Knott, Charlie Charleston, Les Harris, 'Scatty' Yule, Jim Ham, Peter Chivers, Roger Smith (Trainer). Seated: Godfrey Knott, Ron Gillespie, Michael Gallagher, Joe Reed, Lester Linnington.

East Cowes Vics, 1929. Back row, left to right: Cecil Toogood, Jim Hunt, 'Geo' Williams, 'Ern' Lemon, Fred Phillips, Bill Burton, Roy Brown. Centre row: Bill Southcott, 'Blimey' Ballard, Harold Merrifield, Frank Moore, 'Pe' Vine. Front row: Bill Chiverton, Fred Lloyd, Harry Geeg, 'Ern' Pryer, Tom Saunders.

I have been unable to discover much detail regarding this reserve team for the East Cowes Vics, for the season of 1909/10.

Runners-up, Baring Shield, Grange Road Football Team, 1920. Back row, left to right: Bob Roy, Cyril Board, Wilf Kemp, William Wright, Mr Hallis. Centre row: Ernest Nobbs, John Tee, Lionel Ballard. Front row: Douglas Aitken, Percy Woodford, Alfred Sinnicks, Albert Smith, Leonard Sibbick.

EAST COWES:
YOUTH GROUPS

The Boys Brigade string duo.

The East Cowes Junior Red Cross, summer 1953. Back row, left to right: Brenda Abrook, Maureen Jones, Mary Steele, Val Attrill, Josie Little. Front row: Mrs Benson, Yvonne Caws (with the cup), Miss Efford.

The 1st East Cowes Girls Life Brigade fife and drum band, making their first ever appearance at Wootton Carnival, 1930. Some of those pictured are Lillian Halliday (Captain), Miriam Fleming and Rosie Coated (side drummers), Mr Sinnicks (bass drum), Lou Woodford (little girl in uniform), Win Barnes, Freda Slade, May Summer and Marjory Slade.

The 1st East Cowes Girls Life Brigade at a garden party, 1928. This was held at the home of Elsie James, who lived in Cambridge Road, and was the President of the unit until she died aged 101. Back row, left to right: Lilian Baird, Lillian Halliday (Captain), Mrs Waite. Third row: Win Barnes, Marjory Slade, Win Barton, Mavis Love, Lily Smith, Kath Lawrence, Elsie Howes, Dorothy Moore, Eileen Lawrence, Olive Lowein, Ivy Ackland, Clarice Edwards. Second row: Hilda Adams, Mabel Adams, Agnes Crozier, Joy Knight, Mrs Amy Fryer (President), Margery Fleming, Gladys Bell, May Bettridge. Front row: Olive Merrifield, Lena Guttridge, Ethel Gnazell, Beattie Dove, Barbara Lawrence, Mary Trevis, Ena Barton, Doris Attwater, Mabel Saunders.

The Boys Brigade Band with their minister, the Revd J.H. Fisher, at Adelaide Grove Methodist Church, 1946.

When not involved with band work, the company would often attend camp. This photograph is from the official summer camp held at Glynde, Surrey, in 1946.

The Boys Brigade was formed in 1916 but lapsed due to the First World War. It was re-formed in 1920, with the band frequently playing a large part in the Brigade's work.

The wedding of Harold Thorne to Margery Fleming at East Cowes Wesleyan Church, Adelaide Grove, 15 August 1940. The bride was a member of the Girls Life Brigade and the groom a serving fireman. Both organizations provided the archway of honour. Some of those pictured are Rose Phillips (groom's aunt) Mr Barton (fireman), Beryl Douglas (GLB member), Harold Thorne (groom), Margery Fleming (bride), Betty Tiltman (GLB member) and Ernest Catley (fireman).

The Boys Brigade annual inspection, East Cowes Town Hall. 'Skipper' Gutteridge, captain of this unit, had the distinction of holding that position from 1926 to 1977 – fifty-one years.

The Boys Brigade again enjoying summer camp at Bracklesham Bay in Sussex, 1958.

In 1921 the East Cowes Sea Scouts decided to hold a camp in France. Those who went are pictured with Uffa Fox (centre, wearing cap) next to their whaler on East Cowes beach.

Under the tuition of Uffa Fox they received final instructions in the preparation for their journey.

It was customary that apprentices at Saunders Roe performed a play on completion of their term. They are seen here with their production of *Seagulls Over Sorrento* in 1956. Standing, left to right: Dave Halliday, Roger Kearin, Peter Hockton, Rosemary ?, Peter Dean, Dennis Thomas, Tony Jones, Derek Ashwood, Sue Hickman, Veronica Brading. Seated: Jeremy Hazzard.

ROYAL OSBORNE

Queen Victoria seated in the stern of her Royal

Yacht at Trinity landing stage, before sailing over

to the mainland.

This is believed to be one of the last photographs taken of Queen Victoria, and dates from 1900 – one year before her death. The Queen first visited the Island in 1831, when she was Princess Victoria, accompanied by her mother HRH Duchess of Kent. They stayed at Norris Castle and the Princess performed her first public engagement, that of laying the foundation stone of East Cowes Church.

Louise Way, on the right, served Princess Beatrice at Osborne Cottage. Elizabeth Hudson served the Munshi Hafry Abdul Karrin at Arthurs Cottage. Mary Anne Hewer was a friend of both ladies. Louise Way and Elizabeth Hudson both saw Queen Victoria on her deathbed in 1901.

Not long after her marriage in 1840 Queen Victoria, inconvenienced by the rudeness and familiarity of those in Brighton, purchased from Lady Isabella Blachford an estate of 1,000 acres on the Isle of Wight. The house was pulled down and the first stone of the pavilion wing of Osborne House was laid by the Queen and Prince Consort on 23 June 1845. Beneath the spot selected for the cornerstone of the building was deposited a glass bottle containing a complete set of coins of her reign. The house was completed and occupied by September 1846.

Osborne House and estate was privately owned by Queen Victoria, having been purchased with her own private purse. During her married life the royal household would be resident from 18 July to 23 August and again from 18 December until 23 February. This ensured that they were in residence during the yachting and Christmas seasons. The building is in the Palladian style, and resembles an Italian villa. The campanile is 100 feet high.

East Cowes is the headquarters of Trinity House service for the south coast and it was here that a royal landing stage was constructed for Queen Victoria and members of her family. The royal shelter was moved to Hogan Road in Newport and converted into a bungalow in 1922.

The Royal Naval College at Osborne was the naval training establishment for the Crown Heads and other officer cadets in the 1920s. This shows the ward in the College hospital.

Queen Victoria died on 22 January 1901. Her funeral cortège is seen here passing down York Avenue on its way to Trinity Wharf. After the journey back to the mainland, her body lay in state at Westminster Abbey.

East Cowes Castle, formerly the home of the Gort family and used as a dormitory by British and Canadian troops destined for Normandy. After being empty for many years it was demolished in the late 1960s.

Norris Castle was built for Lord Henry Seymour by the architect Sir J. Wyattville in 1799. The castle stands in a park half a mile east of East Cowes. It was here that the East Cowes Castle of Henry VIII formerly stood. Sir Robert Bell purchased it in 1839 and it was let to HRH Duchess of Kent in 1859, so that she could be near her daughter Queen Victoria.

Another view of East Cowes Castle. The architect, John Nash, took up residence here on his retirement in 1831. All that remains of this fine castle today is the brick ice house.

The south gatehouse to East Cowes Castle, another imposing structure that has now been demolished. Only the boundary pillar remains, hidden by ivy.

Section Eleven

WHIPPINGHAM

*The attractive and historical Whippingham
Church, used for worship by Queen Victoria and
the Royal Family, was designed by Albert, the
Prince Consort. It overlooks the River Medina,
and stands on the site of the original church, built
by William the Conqueror in the eleventh century.*

This church, founded by William Fitz Osborne in 1066, was dedicated in the twelfth century to Mildred, a Saxon princess. It is here that Princess Beatrice and Prince Henry of Battenberg were married and it is the last resting place of the Battenbergs. The ground plan takes the form of a Latin cross and the building comprises a chancel, nave and north and south transepts. The unusual length of the chancel is due to the fact that the Osborne pews are located in it. Opposite the church are the picturesque Victoria and Albert almshouses, erected by the Queen in 1880.

Outside Whippingham Church on 5 February 1896. People wait to pay their last respects to Prince Henry of Battenberg.

The inside of the church decorated and draped for the occasion.

Whippingham School was originally for children of workers on the Royal Estate. As the size of the estate was reduced the school was opened to the general public as well. Seen here are two classes. The picture above dates from 1901, and the class below was photographed in 1914.

Rann's forge at Whippingham has been serving horses and farmers since 1922. Today Trevor Rann continues the business. Frank Rann and his son Bob are pictured outside the forge in 1937.

The Folly Inn started life as a beached barque in 1752 when it was used for the serving of drinks and other refreshments to sailors travelling to Newport Quay. Over the years it has been gradually built up into an inn and until the early 1880s part of the original keel was in the main bar – but someone gave it to a museum and its whereabouts are now unknown. The name 'Folly' is presumed to have been derived from the name of the original barque, *Les Follies*.

Acknowledgements

This book would not have been possible but for the assistance given by many people. Therefore, I would like to thank the following:

All Saints Church, Gurnard • Valerie Attrill • the Revd Paul Bailey (Cowes Baptist Church) • Rosetta Brading • Roy Brinton • Cowes Amateur Operatic and Dramatic Society • H. Denham • East Cowes Heritage Centre Mrs J. Fripp • Mr Gould • Grange Road School, East Cowes J. Groves • E. Guttridge • Mrs B. Harvey • Brian Harwood 'Chick' Hickling • Cllr R. Hilton • T.C. Hudson • J. Isham (Cowes Fire Brigade) • P. Jeffrey • Malcolm Johnson • Colin Leal • David Line Graham Lloyd (Funeral Director, Cowes) • G.K. Moreton • P. Morris • Andrew Munn Northwood Cricket Club • Mrs M. Pickering • A. Polino (Roma Taxis, Newport) • the Revd M. Purbrick (Cowes Roman Catholic Church) Phoebe Raddings • J.H. Reed • Miss P. Richmond • Salvation Army, Cowes C. Sibbick • P. South • Vera Taylor • Westland Aerospace • Whippingham School • Mr and Mrs J. Woods • Mr and Mrs Wray.

I would especially like to acknowledge the help given in the preparation of this book by my friends Bert Draper, Wayne Pritchett (Harbour Master, Newport) and Peter T.G. White.

BRITAIN IN OLD PHOTOGRAPHS

To order any of these titles please telephone Littlehampton Book Services on 01903 721596

ALDERNEY

Alderney: A Second Selection, *B Bonnard*

BEDFORDSHIRE

Bedfordshire at Work, *N Lutt*

BERKSHIRE

Maidenhead, *M Hayles & D Hedges*
Around Maidenhead, *M Hayles & B Hedges*
Reading, *P Southerton*
Reading: A Second Selection, *P Southerton*
Sandhurst and Crowthorne, *K Dancy*
Around Slough, *J Hunter & K Hunter*
Around Thatcham, *P Allen*
Around Windsor, *B Hedges*

BUCKINGHAMSHIRE

Buckingham and District, *R Cook*
High Wycombe, *R Goodearl*
Around Stony Stratford, *A Lambert*

CHESHIRE

Cheshire Railways, *M Hitches*
Chester, *S Nichols*

CLWYD

Clwyd Railways, *M Hitches*

CLYDESDALE

Clydesdale, *Lesmahagow Parish Historical Association*

CORNWALL

Cornish Coast, *T Bowden*
Falmouth, *P Gilson*
Lower Fal, *P Gilson*
Around Padstow, *M McCarthy*
Around Penzance, *J Holmes*
Penzance and Newlyn, *J Holmes*
Around Truro, *A Lyne*
Upper Fal, *P Gilson*

CUMBERLAND

Cockermouth and District, *J Bernard Bradbury*
Keswick and the Central Lakes, *J Marsh*
Around Penrith, *F Boyd*
Around Whitehaven, *H Fancy*

DERBYSHIRE

Derby, *D Buxton*
Around Matlock, *D Barton*

DEVON

Colyton and Seaton, *T Gosling*
Dawlish and Teignmouth, *G Gosling*
Devon Aerodromes, *K Saunders*
Exeter, *P Thomas*
Exmouth and Budleigh Salterton, *T Gosling*
From Haldon to Mid-Dartmoor, *T Hall*
Honiton and the Otter Valley, *J Yallop*
Around Kingsbridge, *K Tanner*
Around Seaton and Sidmouth, *T Gosling*
Seaton, Axminster and Lyme Regis, *T Gosling*

DORSET

Around Blandford Forum, *B Cox*
Bournemouth, *M Colman*
Bridport and the Bride Valley, *J Barrell & S Humphries*
Dorchester, *T Gosling*
Around Gillingham, *P Crocker*

DURHAM

Darlington, *G Flynn*
Darlington: A Second Selection, *G Flynn*
Durham People, *M Richardson*
Houghton-le-Spring and Hetton-le-Hole, *K Richardson*
Houghton-le-Spring and Hetton-le-Hole:
    A Second Selection, *K Richardson*
Sunderland, *S Miller & B Bell*
Teesdale, *D Coggins*
Teesdale: A Second Selection, *P Raine*
Weardale, *J Crosby*
Weardale: A Second Selection, *J Crosby*

DYFED

Aberystwyth and North Ceredigion,
    Dyfed Cultural Services Dept
Haverfordwest, *Dyfed Cultural Services Dept*
Upper Tywi Valley, *Dyfed Cultural Services Dept*

ESSEX

Around Grays, *B Evans*

GLOUCESTERSHIRE

Along the Avon from Stratford to Tewkesbury, *J Jeremiah*
Cheltenham: A Second Selection, *R Whiting*
Cheltenham at War, *P Gill*
Cirencester, *J Welsford*
Around Cirencester, *E Cuss & P Griffiths*
Forest, The, *D Mullin*
Gloucester, *J Voyce*
Around Gloucester, *A Sutton*
Gloucester: From the Walwin Collection, *J Voyce*
North Cotswolds, *D Viner*
Severn Vale, *A Sutton*
Stonehouse to Painswick, *A Sutton*
Stroud and the Five Valleys, *S Gardiner & L Padin*
Stroud and the Five Valleys: A Second Selection,
    S Gardiner & L Padin
Stroud's Golden Valley, *S Gardiner & L Padin*
Stroudwater and Thames & Severn Canals,
    E Cuss & S Gardiner
Stroudwater and Thames & Severn Canals: A Second
    Selection, *E Cuss & S Gardiner*
Tewkesbury and the Vale of Gloucester, *C Hilton*
Thornbury to Berkeley, *J Hudson*
Uley, Dursley and Cam, *A Sutton*
Wotton-under-Edge to Chipping Sodbury, *A Sutton*

GWYNEDD

Anglesey, *M Hitches*
Gwynedd Railways, *M Hitches*
Around Llandudno, *M Hitches*
Vale of Conwy, *M Hitches*

HAMPSHIRE

Gosport, *J Sadden*
Portsmouth, *P Rogers & D Francis*

HEREFORDSHIRE

Herefordshire, *A Sandford*

HERTFORDSHIRE

Barnet, *I Norrie*
Hitchin, *A Fleck*
St Albans, *S Mullins*
Stevenage, *M Appleton*

ISLE OF MAN

The Tourist Trophy, *B Snelling*

ISLE OF WIGHT

Newport, *D Parr*
Around Ryde, *D Parr*

JERSEY

Jersey: A Third Selection, *R Lemprière*

KENT

Bexley, *M Scott*
Broadstairs and St Peter's, *J Whyman*
Bromley, Keston and Hayes, *M Scott*
Canterbury: A Second Selection, *D Butler*
Chatham and Gillingham, *P MacDougall*
Chatham Dockyard, *P MacDougall*
Deal, *J Broady*
Early Broadstairs and St Peter's, *B Wootton*
East Kent at War, *D Collyer*
Eltham, *J Kennett*
Folkestone: A Second Selection, *A Taylor & E Rooney*
Goudhurst to Tenterden, *A Guilmant*
Gravesend, *R Hiscock*
Around Gravesham, *R Hiscock & D Grierson*
Herne Bay, *J Hawkins*
Lympne Airport, *D Collyer*
Maidstone, *I Hales*
Margate, *R Clements*
RAF Hawkinge, *R Humphreys*
RAF Manston, *RAF Manston History Club*
RAF Manston: A Second Selection,
    RAF Manston History Club
Ramsgate and Thanet Life, *D Perkins*
Romney Marsh, *E Carpenter*
Sandwich, *C Wanostrocht*
Around Tonbridge, *C Bell*
Tunbridge Wells, *M Rowlands & I Beavis*
Tunbridge Wells: A Second Selection,
    M Rowlands & I Beavis
Around Whitstable, *C Court*
Wingham, Adisham and Littlebourne, *M Crane*

LANCASHIRE

Around Barrow-in-Furness, *J Garbutt & J Marsh*
Blackpool, *C Rothwell*
Bury, *J Hudson*
Chorley and District, *J Smith*
Fleetwood, *C Rothwell*
Heywood, *J Hudson*
Around Kirkham, *C Rothwell*
Lancashire North of the Sands, *J Garbutt & J Marsh*
Around Lancaster, *S Ashworth*
Lytham St Anne's, *C Rothwell*
North Fylde, *C Rothwell*
Radcliffe, *J Hudson*
Rossendale, *B Moore & N Dunnachie*

LEICESTERSHIRE

Around Ashby-de-la-Zouch, *K Hillier*
Charnwood Forest, *I Keil, W Humphrey & D Wix*
Leicester, *D Burton*
Leicester: A Second Selection, *D Burton*
Melton Mowbray, *T Hickman*
Around Melton Mowbray, *T Hickman*
River Soar, *D Wix, P Shacklock & I Keil*
Rutland, *T Clough*
Vale of Belvoir, *T Hickman*
Around the Welland Valley, *S Mastoris*

LINCOLNSHIRE

Grimsby, *J Tierney*
Around Grimsby, *J Tierney*
Grimsby Docks, *J Tierney*
Lincoln, *D Cuppleditch*

Scunthorpe, *D Taylor*
Skegness, *W Kime*
Around Skegness, *W Kime*

LONDON

Balham and Tooting, *P Loobey*
Crystal Palace, Penge & Anerley, *M Scott*
Greenwich and Woolwich, *K Clark*
Hackney: A Second Selection, *D Mander*
Lewisham and Deptford, *J Coulter*
Lewisham and Deptford: A Second Selection, *J Coulter*
Streatham, *P Loobey*
Around Whetstone and North Finchley, *J Heathfield*
Woolwich, *B Evans*

MONMOUTHSHIRE

Chepstow and the River Wye, *A Rainsbury*
Monmouth and the River Wye, *Monmouth Museum*

NORFOLK

Great Yarmouth, *M Teun*
Norwich, *M Colman*
Wymondham and Attleborough, *P Yaxley*

NORTHAMPTONSHIRE

Around Stony Stratford, *A Lambert*

NOTTINGHAMSHIRE

Arnold and Bestwood, *M Spick*
Arnold and Bestwood: A Second Selection, *M Spick*
Changing Face of Nottingham, *G Oldfield*
Mansfield, *Old Mansfield Society*
Around Newark, *T Warner*
Nottingham: 1944–1974, *D Whitworth*
Sherwood Forest, *D Ottewell*
Victorian Nottingham, *M Payne*

OXFORDSHIRE

Around Abingdon, *P Horn*
Banburyshire, *M Barnett & S Gosling*
Burford, *A Jewell*
Around Didcot and the Hagbournes, *B Lingham*
Garsington, *M Gunther*
Around Henley-on-Thames, *S Ellis*
Oxford: The University, *J Rhodes*
Thame to Watlington, *N Hood*
Around Wallingford, *D Beasley*
Witney, *T Worley*
Around Witney, *C Mitchell*
Witney District, *T Worley*
Around Woodstock, *J Bond*

POWYS

Brecon, *Brecknock Museum*
Welshpool, *E Bredsdorff*

SHROPSHIRE

Shrewsbury, *D Trumper*
Whitchurch to Market Drayton, *M Morris*

SOMERSET

Bath, *J Hudson*
Bridgwater and the River Parrett, *R Fitzhugh*
Bristol, *D Moorcroft & N Campbell-Sharp*
Changing Face of Keynsham,
    B Lowe & M Whitehead

Chard and Ilminster, *G Gosling & F Huddy*
Crewkerne and the Ham Stone Villages,
    G Gosling & F Huddy
Around Keynsham and Saltford, *B Lowe & T Brown*
Midsomer Norton and Radstock, *C Howell*
Somerton, Ilchester and Langport, *G Gosling & F Huddy*
Taunton, *N Chipchase*
Around Taunton, *N Chipchase*
Wells, *C Howell*
Weston-Super-Mare, *S Poole*
Around Weston-Super-Mare, *S Poole*
West Somerset Villages, *K Houghton & L Thomas*

STAFFORDSHIRE

Aldridge, *J Farrow*
Bilston, *E Rees*
Black Country Transport: Aviation, *A Brew*
Around Burton upon Trent, *G Sowerby & R Farman*
Bushbury, *A Chatwin, M Mills & E Rees*
Around Cannock, *M Mills & S Belcher*
Around Leek, *R Poole*
Lichfield, *H Clayton & K Simmons*
Around Pattingham and Wombourne, *M Griffiths,*
    P Leigh & M Mills
Around Rugeley, *T Randall & J Anslow*
Smethwick, *J Maddison*
Stafford, *J Anslow & T Randall*
Around Stafford, *J Anslow & T Randall*
Stoke-on-Trent, *I Lawley*
Around Tamworth, *R Sulima*
Around Tettenhall and Codsall, *M Mills*
Tipton, Wednesbury and Darlaston, *R Pearson*
Walsall, *D Gilbert & M Lewis*
Wednesbury, *I Bott*
West Bromwich, *R Pearson*

SUFFOLK

Ipswich: A Second Selection, *D Kindred*
Around Ipswich, *D Kindred*
Around Mildenhall, *C Dring*
Southwold to Aldeburgh, *H Phelps*
Around Woodbridge, *H Phelps*

SURREY

Cheam and Belmont, *P Berry*
Croydon, *S Bligh*
Dorking and District, *K Harding*
Around Dorking, *A Jackson*
Around Epsom, *P Berry*
Farnham: A Second Selection, *J Parratt*
Around Haslemere and Hindhead, *T Winter & G Collyer*
Richmond, *Richmond Local History Society*
Sutton, *P Berry*

SUSSEX

Arundel and the Arun Valley, *J Godfrey*
Bishopstone and Seaford, *P Pople & P Berry*
Brighton and Hove, *J Middleton*
Brighton and Hove: A Second Selection, *J Middleton*
Around Crawley, *M Goldsmith*
Hastings, *P Haines*
Hastings: A Second Selection, *P Haines*
Around Haywards Heath, *J Middleton*
Around Heathfield, *A Gillet & B Russell*
Around Heathfield: A Second Selection,
    A Gillet & B Russell
High Weald, *B Harwood*
High Weald: A Second Selection, *B Harwood*
Horsham and District, *T Wales*

Lewes, *J Middleton*
RAF Tangmere, *A Saunders*
Around Rye, *A Dickinson*
Around Worthing, *S White*

WARWICKSHIRE

Along the Avon from Stratford to Tewkesbury, *J Jeremiah*
Bedworth, *J Burton*
Coventry, *D McGrory*
Around Coventry, *D McGrory*
Nuneaton, *S Clews & S Vaughan*
Around Royal Leamington Spa, *J Cameron*
Around Royal Leamington Spa: A Second Selection,
    J Cameron
Around Warwick, *R Booth*

WESTMORLAND

Eden Valley, *J Marsh*
Kendal, *M & P Duff*
South Westmorland Villages, *J Marsh*
Westmorland Lakes, *J Marsh*

WILTSHIRE

Around Amesbury, *P Daniels*
Chippenham and Lacock, *A Wilson & M Wilson*
Around Corsham and Box, *A Wilson & M Wilson*
Around Devizes, *D Buxton*
Around Highworth, *G Tanner*
Around Highworth and Faringdon, *G Tanner*
Around Malmesbury, *A Wilson*
Marlborough: A Second Selection, *P Colman*
Around Melksham,
    Melksham and District Historical Association
Nadder Valley, *R. Sawyer*
Salisbury, *P Saunders*
Salisbury: A Second Selection, *P Daniels*
Salisbury: A Third Selection, *P Daniels*
Around Salisbury, *P Daniels*
Swindon: A Third Selection, *The Swindon Society*
Swindon: A Fourth Selection, *The Swindon Society*
Trowbridge, *M Marshman*
Around Wilton, *P Daniels*
Around Wootton Bassett, Cricklade and Purton, *T Sharp*

WORCESTERSHIRE

Evesham to Bredon, *F Archer*
Around Malvern, *K Smith*
Around Pershore, *M Dowty*
Redditch and the Needle District, *R Saunders*
Redditch: A Second Selection, *R Saunders*
Around Tenbury Wells, *D Green*
Worcester, *M Dowty*
Around Worcester, *R Jones*
Worcester in a Day, *M Dowty*
Worcestershire at Work, *R Jones*

YORKSHIRE

Huddersfield: A Second Selection, *H Wheeler*
Huddersfield: A Third Selection, *H Wheeler*
Leeds Road and Rail, *R Vickers*
Pontefract, *R van Riel*
Scarborough, *D Coggins*
Scarborough's War Years, *R Percy*
Skipton and the Dales, *Friends of the Craven Museum*
Around Skipton-in-Craven, *Friends of the Craven Museum*
Yorkshire Wolds, *I & M Sumner*